THE STORY
OF THE BUDDHA

The

STORY

of

the BUDDHA

JOHN TARRANT

SHAMBHALA

Shambhala Publications, Inc.
2129 13th Street
Boulder, Colorado 80302
www.shambhala.com

A section of this work was published in a slightly different form in *Lion's Roar* magazine.
Translations from Buddhist texts are by Joan Sutherland and John Tarrant and are reprinted
from the Pacific Zen School private koan-study curriculum by permission of the translators.

Cover art: "Lotus Sutra, Chapters 12 and 14," Mary Griggs Burke Collection, Gift of the
Mary and Jackson Burke Foundation, 2015.
Cover design: Daniel Urban-Brown
Interior design: Kate E. White

9 8 7 6 5 4 3 2 1

First Edition
Printed in China

Shambhala Publications makes every effort to print on acid-free, recycled paper.
Shambhala Publications is distributed worldwide by Penguin Random House, Inc.,
and its subsidiaries.

LIBRARY OF CONGRESS CATALOGING-IN-PUBLICATION DATA
Names: Tarrant, John, 1949- author.
Title: The story of the Buddha / John Tarrant.
Identifiers: LCCN 2023048069 | ISBN 9781645473138 (hardcover)
Subjects: LCSH: Gautama Buddha—Biography. | Buddhism—History.
Classification: LCC BQ882 .T37 2024 | DDC 294.3/63—dc23/eng/20231025
LC record available at https://lccn.loc.gov/2023048069

for Allison

CONTENTS

THE STORY
OF THE BUDDHA

INTRODUCTION

In the beginning, there was silence and nontime—the universe had not yet begun. But even silence is a step. It repeats, it's the beginning of a journey.

At the time of our story the universe had acquired many features and forms of life, but there were still gaps in the sequence of time, gaps that were left over from the beginning.

In those gaps strange things happened: spirits and beings from other realms worked openly together to shape the fate of humans; a dream of a white elephant made a woman pregnant; horses wept; the Lord of the Demons was lonely; it wasn't hard to recall previous lives; and a Black Snake Dragon King could remember what had happened in a previous universe.

In the beginning, there was silence and nontime—the universe had not yet begun.

Perhaps the story really begins with this mysterious Black Snake Dragon King.

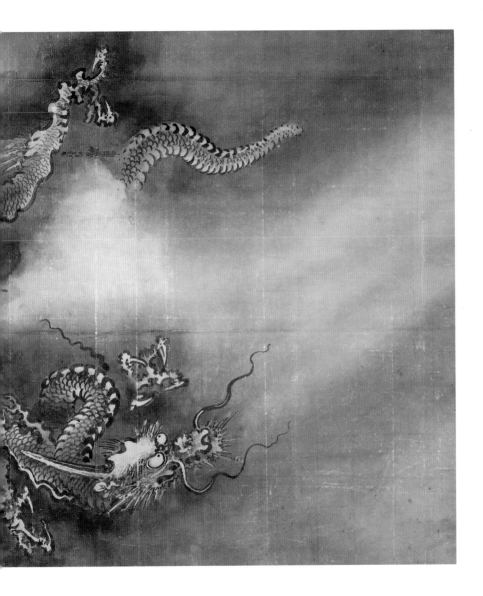

Perhaps the story really begins with this mysterious Black Snake Dragon King, who barely notices whether we are in a universe or in the nontime between universes. Meanwhile this dragon lives in a pool at the foot of a waterfall in a great forest.

The story moves ahead when the queen, who became pregnant in a dream and had great joy of her pregnancy, died shortly after the birth. The child, a boy, survived. In his grief, the old king grasped his kingdom with hands like claws. All news and evidence of sickness, old age, and death was hidden from his son.

The prince was raised inside this illusion and struggled to find his way out. There were forces who wished him well and forces who tried to conceal his true situation. It is still hard to tell which of these was which.

The prince left home on his great white horse in the dead of night, the very night his own child was born. In this way he forsook everyone he loved and, as an afterthought, all that he owned. In his understanding, he had to approach what he longed for by losing everything.

As a child in the clean, warm public library in Launceston,
Tasmania, I stumbled from the Egyptians into the Greeks
and found that my life could pour itself into myths, more
or less involuntarily. In his black ship, Odysseus visited
the world of the dead, and Persephone was carried off,
lamenting, and ate the pomegranate seeds that, for part
of every year, bound her to winter and the underworld.
Every night I wiped the condensation from my bedroom
window and regarded the town below and the lights of the
cars passing occasionally across the hillside. Through the
company of the Greek stories, my own abductions and night
journeys became possible. The stories sustained me during
the long hours at school.

Odysseus tried to evade conscription into the Trojan
War because he wanted to remain with everyone and
everything he loved, as the king of a not very wealthy island.
He spent the next twenty years struggling to get back to his
palace. He wanted wine, roast pig, figs, and the taste of the

dust of his native land. Most of all, he longed to hold in his arms and in his gaze someone who knew him and knew his story; he wanted the blessing of someone who loved him, of his Penelope, and also of his old dog, his childhood nurse, his son, and his father. That blessing was greater than wealth or power.

If we pour ourselves into the story of the Buddha, it is a myth with a very different trajectory. We enter the journey from an unusual place as far as myths go: we begin where the *Odyssey* ends. The Buddha already has his palace, and everything that can be wanted, along with a wife and a child. He is not hungry or mistreated by a stepmother, his father is not absent, he is not a younger son, war has not come to his lands. And, in spite of his wealth and ease, he is suffocating. His discontent is not merely a recognition of the human condition but a raw suffering and desire, an impetus to see, to see through, to see into, to see exactly. This means to look at the world but also and especially to investigate the mind. All journeys have some tendrils dangling down into the inner life, but now the inwardness is explicit: Understanding is the goal.

And in this quest, the vector of desire is reversed: The taboo thing—the disguised, thrilling, secret thing—is suffering. The prince's task is to draw back the veil behind which the trinity of sickness, old age, and death is hidden and to find that there is a fourth door, which leads into the spiritual path.

Because he was a prince and knew a great deal about acquiring things, the Buddha began by subtraction. He shed his newborn child, his wife, his father, the woman who raised him, his palace, his clothes, his jewelry, his sword, his horse, his best friend, and his food. He turned toward poverty, hunger, and doing without. After that it became a wisdom path to look closely at suffering and death. Pilgrims meditated in graveyards, and hospices became places of discovery.

The prince began to listen to silence. He thought the blessing bestowed by the queen, his mother, might still exist somewhere inside the world.

As the story turned inward, more questions appeared: "Who am I?"; "What do I really, really want?"; "How do I know, and feel, my life?"; "Why do we die?"; "Does consciousness depend on having a body?"; "Is the universe itself conscious or is consciousness some kind of addition late in the game?"—and, hidden inside these questions, "Nevertheless, how can we love life and each other?" The journey is, in an explicit way, about the nature of mind, and of consciousness, and this gives it a special place in the human legacy.

The Buddha investigated the mind with meditation, wonder, questioning, and helpless persistence. After him, people went into their own hearts to look; they stepped into the silence in which the beginning was still present. You could find the gaps inside anything. Every event and every object had these gaps, and when you rested there, you found a place before loss or death and before a need for healing. From this primordial openness everything seemed to flower; the emptiness itself had a vast imagination. But you couldn't take yourself with you.

"What is this?" you wondered, and that became the practice and held you through the journey. You didn't have to be anything or anyone, you just took a step. The whole point of being yourself was a kind of wizardry to avoid entering the silence and being touched by it. This became clear to the

Buddha when he realized that he was not composed of his thoughts. He could resolve things by settling into the gaps between thoughts, and really this was just the mind resting in its own being. The world is always unmaking itself to reveal itself. So any direction he took might lead to the treasure, especially the direction he did not plan to take.

The Buddha's story is full of reversals. Because of the heartbreaking way the prince stole out of the palace on the day his child was born, the path always has an element of refusal—it's not this and also not the next thing. Fame, sex, wealth, familial happiness are all points of departure. They are in the category of "not this."

The next implication is that when we realize that suffering occurs in the midst of happiness, we might in turn realize that happiness can appear unexpectedly in a place where we anticipated suffering. A reversal happens in which "not this" means a life not maintained by make-believe.

If you want to wake up from a dream, every direction you think of takes you deeper into the dream. The Buddha tried many paths and eventually noticed that even his

It's easy to notice how anger narrows us and how despair implies a firm belief in a predictable future.

sacrifices were a kind of bargaining in which he hoped to exchange suffering for wisdom. While he poured his efforts into seeking, he hadn't really left the palace he was raised in.

It's not so hard to work out what we want to escape from in our minds. It's easy to notice how anger narrows us and how despair implies a firm belief in a predictable future. Empires and dominions fail, and that includes the dominion of the self and who we imagine we are. What we step into is stranger; we step into a not knowing.

Freedom is not a copy of something; it is not already known—it is less conceivable than all other conditions. One person sets off on the journey and a different person arrives. The Buddha found that he had been changed because he jumped out of the story he lived by. Later the Chinese Chan masters offered images of effortless wandering as a way to illustrate the paradox that reaching for something gets in the way of what we are reaching for. One of them said, "I went out following the scented grass, and came back chasing falling flowers."[1] There is a happiness that doesn't come from desire or fear or even from being careful with your mind.

Eventually the prince gave up and just sat with his curiosity, a feeling for what was happening and his question, "What is this?" There is an innocence in approaching the quest in this way, and perhaps it is the true beginning of practice. Not understanding was the promising direction. The earth held him up. He saw that even the demons were secretly on his side. The Buddha concluded that the pursuit of the objects of desire meant an endless, violent repetition of his original loss. He passed on to his son the dark gift of being an orphan.

After Siddhartha's long, desperate fast, Sujata the milkmaid, instructed by a dream, appears. Siddhartha drinks the sweet milk rice she offers. With Sujata and her milk, a countermovement begins. She is the muse of the meditation story and brings the blessing and embrace of the world. She holds the healing power of dreams, of food, of rest, acceptance, encouragement—the power of the queen who died. The Buddha himself doesn't want anything enough to be able to transgress. But without desire the story can't move ahead. Sujata gives us what we need to survive the demons of the night.

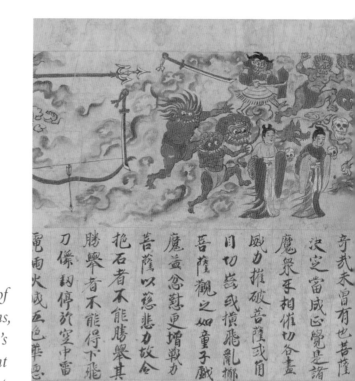

奇我未曾有也菩薩
決定當成正覺是諸
魔眾手相推切咬盡
威力摧破菩薩或甪
目切嵌武損飛亂擲
菩薩觀之如童子戲
魔益忿懟更增戰力
菩薩以慈悲力故令
抱石者不能勝舉其
勝舉者不能得下飛
刀儌鉤停於空中雷
電雨火咸五色華惡

Mara, Lord of the Demons, carries life's ability to torment and distract.

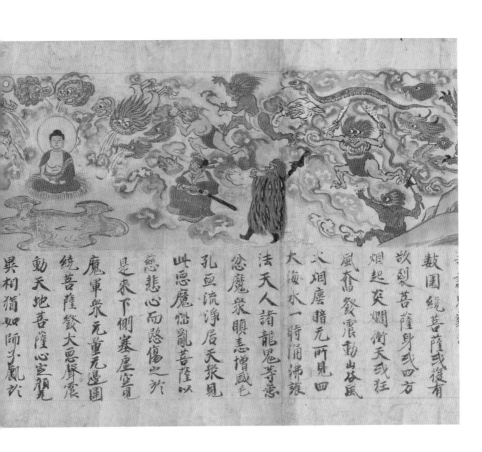

數圍繞菩薩或復有

故裂菩薩身或四方

烟起突爛衝天或狂

風奮發震動山谷風

火炯磨暗无所見四

大海水一時漰沸躁

法天人諸龍鬼莘慈

恣魔衆瞋恚增感毛

孔血流淨居天衆見

此惡魔惱亂菩薩以

慈悲心而愍傷之於

是來下側塞虛空覺

魔軍衆无量无邊圍

繞菩薩發大惡聲震

動天地菩薩心宣顧見

異相猶如師子亂於

Other great forces are interested in Siddhartha's progress. Mara, Lord of the Demons, carries life's ability to torment and distract: the hindrances in the heart—our greed and envy, the cravings and storms of feeling that accumulate painfully, our self-dislike and shame about our greed and envy, along with our ability to be distracted by everything. He is everything that we have pretended, or hoped, that we are not. Mara is also fate, the things that happen to us, such as disease, accident, and bad luck; and the painful things that happen in the world, such as war, famine, children dying, vain and heartless leaders. In Mara's vast army, no two creatures have the same weapons, and even the gods who've promised to protect us flee before them. Mara's secret weakness is that he is lonely, he wants a friend. He too, though unconsciously, is part of the scheme to awaken the prince; even he wants to be loved, and he too can be loved.

Gateways to a larger life are usually to be found where we don't look, otherwise the passages would already be known and in use. I like to imagine them as concealed, written in runes visible only by moonlight. But they are usually hidden in plain sight, guarded by No Trespassing signs. The signs don't say "Avoid this place"; they say "This place is really uninteresting, and even to think about it is tiring and disturbing."

I've spent a lot of time sitting late at night, under a friendly apricot tree, listening to the sound of an owl's wings, of a plane passing over, headed for somewhere important to those who are traveling. I feel the Earth turn, watch the garden, which is a boat that moonlight fills. The border collie sits quietly beside me. To meditate is to show up for the life that we have. In the deep watches of the night, it's not hard to let go of yourself and be at peace.

Finally, just reading the story of the Buddha, I'm in an ancient lineage, and the old grand masters of that lineage look over me and smile and wish us all well. As well as old masters, there are dragons and gods. Telling a story like the Buddha's might bring our attention into their territory. It's good to have their company.

The STORY
of the BUDDHA

It is early in December, winter is coming on, snow is falling lightly in the mountains, and the mind begins to empty. Sit close to the fire and listen while I tell the story.

Long ago and far away, at Lumbini, in the green foothills of the Himalayas, there lived a queen. Her name was Maha Maya, which means "great dream." Her eyes were the color of lotus leaves, her glance was a blessing, and her smile was a gift. After twenty years, she and the king had no child. Then, one midsummer day, she herself handed out gifts to

The queen dreamed that the guardians of the four directions, the great spirits who protect the wisdom teachings, came to her.

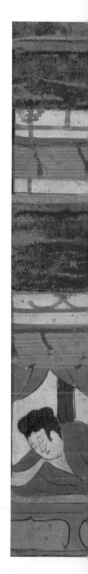

the poor and the hermits. That night under the full moon, everything changed.

The queen dreamed that the guardians of the four directions, the great spirits who protect the wisdom teachings, came to her. They had strong dark faces; they bent over her and carried her high into the mountains. Their wives bathed her in a lake and bore her into a golden palace on Silver Hill, where they laid her down upon a couch. From the steppes and the northern snows, a white elephant with six tusks approached. She could see the wrinkles in his skin. Holding a white lotus in his trunk, he entered her body and disappeared into her womb.

Trees blossomed, musical instruments played by themselves, and people spoke kindly to one another. The old gods, Brahma and Indra, were the witnesses. When the queen awoke, she knew straight away that she had conceived.

In the palace, the dream readers came in red and saffron costumes and considered Maha Maya's dream. The dream readers were analyzing the dream of the queen but also the dream of the universe, which had made this dream.

"He has lived many lives before this one," they said. "He will be a great leader." The king listened but said nothing.

In May when everything is in flower and the birds are singing, Maya's time was near, and she traveled back to her original family, revisiting her childhood places. Her sister, Mahaprajapati, went with her, and when they reached the Lumbini forest, they stopped to rest. The women went into the groves to walk once more among the flowering sal trees, where they had played as children.

Maya climbed into the roots of a great tree. She reached up for a flowering branch, and the branch bowed down to her hand. As she held the bough, her labor began and her child was born.

His skin was golden, and the moment after birth he took seven steps. With one hand he pointed to the sky and with the other to the earth, saying, "Above heaven and beneath the earth, there is only I, eldest and first, alone and sacred."

"Above heaven and beneath the earth, there is only I, eldest and first, alone and sacred."

A soft rain fell, wrapping him in quiet; shadows and wings angled among the branches. Taking him up in their great, awkward claws, dragons bathed him in forest waters. Then the party headed back for home.

At the palace, a rishi—a poet and seer—was waiting. She had learned of the birth by signs and dreams. She had traveled day and night to see the child. She bent over him for a long time, and when she stood up, tears ran down her cheeks. "I'm crying," said the rishi, "I'm old, I won't live to hear him teach."

The queen didn't recover from childbirth; she sank and sank into another world and after a week she died.

After the funeral, the queen's sister, Mahaprajapati, in turn married the king and adopted the child as her own. The boy was named Siddhartha; his family name was Gautama.

The king, still in mourning clothes, gathered the omen readers and fortune tellers.

The chief fortune teller spoke first: "Auspicious signs found on this child's body, such as its golden color and the exquisite radiance that shines from his face, show that he has a branching path before him. If he follows a life of power and splendor, nothing will be denied to him—he will become the emperor of the Earth. That is one path.

"If, on the other hand, he follows the spiritual life, he will go into the forest to search for enlightenment. He'll find what he is looking for on that path, too, and become the founder of a great tradition that will help everyone toward freedom from the suffering that the mind inflicts."

"What conditions," asked the king, "would lead this boy to take the path in which he will become the emperor of the Earth with its plains and fertile valleys, its cities, towers, and armies? And what conditions might lead him to forget his ambitions and responsibilities and seek enlightenment?"

"Great king, it's clear. His natural course will be to seek freedom of the mind, freedom from the chains of suffering, and freedom for all creatures. Four things, four sights, four touches, four meetings will turn him away from ruling. It will be hard to prevent these occurrences. And if he sees these four sights, there will be no turning back."

"And what might these four events, four sights, four touches, four blows consist of?" wondered the king.

"That too is clear. The first sight is to see someone old and decrepit, long in the tooth, feeble, and short of breath. That is the first touch."

"I see," said the king. "And the second?"

"The next sight is someone sick, fevered, coughing up blood, and in a bad way. That would have a powerful effect."

"Go on," the king's voice was hoarse.

The wise men began to speak more quickly: "Your Majesty, the third sight, yes, well that's a corpse, we're certain of it, to be sure—a body laid out and ready for burning.

"The fourth touch—and no doubt Your Majesty has guessed this—well, that is the sight of a person who seeks the way, someone who has forsaken ambition in the world and is indifferent to the favor of others or the things that everyone desires, indifferent even to their own thoughts and passions. A glimpse of that kind of person and the prince would surely leave the kingdom."

The next day the palace was closed off and the child sequestered, shut off from the four forbidden sights.

* * *

Siddhartha's childhood was as cushioned and unremarkable as his minders could make it. Years later, though, he remembered an incident that was significant. In the memory, his father, the king, is breaking a furrow in the fields during the annual plowing ceremony. The oxen have a comforting, animal smell, and flower garlands are strung on their horns. Siddhartha is a child, not quite school age. He lies under a rose apple tree, alone for a moment, unattended. His father is absorbed in his task, and his minders are watching the ceremony; the child is held in no one's gaze. A light breeze touches his face, there is dappled shade and the scent of grass. His eyes move slowly over the paddock. Nothing is on his mind. There is no fear, no tension, no desire.

A parakeet flies into the green branches and the sky opens before it and closes behind it, fitting exactly. His breath opens and closes, too. Time stops, the sun stands still in the sky, he is sheltered in the leafy twilight. There is nothing to add, no resistance to strip away; everything is complete and sufficient.

A question appears in his mind, the way a bird appears in the sky. The question is "Am I afraid of this happiness?" and makes no sense to the child. As well as a question, it's the beginning of a fear, a doubt held up against completeness and the demands that such completeness might make. This fear also tells him who he is, pulls him down into who he is—a child in a field.

Then the spell breaks, the sun begins to move again, and the palace attendants remember the boy under the tree, swooping down to feed him milk rice. He returns to luxury, forgetfulness, impatience, beautiful things, and beautiful manners. He returns to existing at a distance from his life.

Other things happened. He had a cousin who liked to hunt, and one afternoon winged a swan with an arrow. Siddhartha got to the bird first, and she was still alive. He saw the fear in her eyes, felt her shaking run up his arm into his own body. She was like him, he thought—she wanted to live and go back to her swan life with her mate and cygnets. He was touched by her: "Everything alive," he thought, "has its own truth." He broke the arrow, pulled the shaft through, stroked the swan's soft neck, and wrapped her to his chest. He kept the bird till its wing healed and he could release it. This enraged his cousin, but Siddhartha didn't care. After that the cousin hated him.

Whenever the prince went to town, men on horseback hurried ahead to clear the streets. The poor were driven down side alleys, the sick and the old were thrust through the nearest doorway, funerals were interrupted, and wandering pilgrims were ordered to conceal themselves. By the time the prince came through, no blemish marred what he saw. He began to notice that he didn't fit in. He was a lonely child.

He chose for a best friend his chariot driver, someone he met every day, a boy named Channa. When you saw one of them, the other was somewhere near. Channa knew the hidden pathways, the existence of which had never

The eyes didn't ask for anything,
and their steadiness was disturbing.

爾時太子出城南門見一病人問因緣時

occurred to Siddhartha, and they sneaked out of the palace unsupervised. The gods conspired with them, making the guards drowsy and distracted.

The first time the young men went into the city together, someone appeared in front of them—a woman ancient and bent over from work in the fields. Her hair was thin and white and floated in cloudlike wisps; her skin was like dark, cracked clay, and her cheeks were sunken. He couldn't help staring, and she felt his gaze and turned her head like a bird to look up at him. Her black eyes held his. She was like nothing he had ever seen, and her eyes were open to him. He felt for a moment that he had stepped outside of the dream he was always inside. He turned to touch his friend, but when he turned back, the woman had disappeared.

Four times the two friends went into the town, and each time they met someone strange.

On the second journey, Siddhartha stepped into a shop thinking it was a place to get something to drink, and as his eyes adjusted, he saw a figure on a bed by the wall.

The man was thin and sweating, the bones in his face stood out, he was shaking and talking to himself. He coughed and blood came out of his mouth. Again the man's eyes caught his. The eyes didn't ask for anything, and their steadiness was disturbing.

Siddhartha's friend called out and the prince stumbled outside. When he turned back to the shop, he couldn't find the man.

"What was that? What is happening to him?" asked Siddhartha. Channa shrugged, and the prince realized that, if his friend had seen the man, he would have found nothing remarkable about this sight. The meeting was for Siddhartha alone. The prince wondered, with the dizziness of someone on a precipice, why he had asked.

On the third journey, a day blue and unshadowed, they were returning at dusk when four men ran by carrying a litter. They held torches in their hands and as they drew level with the boys, they stopped. The litter held a bundle in white linen. As in a dream, one of the men carefully wound back the cloth and uncovered the face for the boys to see. It was a young woman. There was nothing disfigured about her face; it was just that no breath moved through her. Her green eyes were open. Under the gaze of the bearers the prince's hand rose slowly to touch her cheek; her silence and the shocking chill of her skin was something he remembered all his life.

Channa was concerned. "You know about this though, right?" It was not that Siddhartha didn't know about death; he knew his mother had died. But these facts had had no weight with him before. He felt as if he were struggling up from sleep.

On their fourth trip outside the palace, the boys ran into a woman in robes, a pilgrim. "Who are you?" Siddhartha asked. "What are you doing?"

She laughed, amused by them, amused by everything. When they persisted, she said that she was a traveler, like clouds, like the river. Siddhartha felt hurt. He had hoped she would explain things, that she might end his confusion right then. "Well, someone has to put an end to suffering," she said, and laughed again as if they were sharing a joke. But he took from that meeting the idea that a journey was required.

It's said that the gods intervened and themselves took the form of the forbidden sights—immortals becoming illustrations of mortality. It is also said that the spirit of the prince's birth mother, Maha Maya, was watching from above, touching events, moving the conditions, entering the pilgrim's body.

That was the prince's last encounter with gods in disguise. The sights disturbed his dreams. He became absent-minded during his mathematics classes. He began to wonder what was behind the obvious things he saw.

Eventually he married a girl called Yasodhara. The wedding was in midsummer and flowers and more flowers were thrown over them. They were cousins who had been born on the same day, and the astrologers told Yasodhara that she had great things in store, too. The cousins saw each other every day—Yasodhara wore men's clothes to go riding with Siddhartha, and at night she played music.

Yasodhara was a person who saw into people. Siddhartha wanted things without knowing what they were, was waking up from a dream that had been sealed around

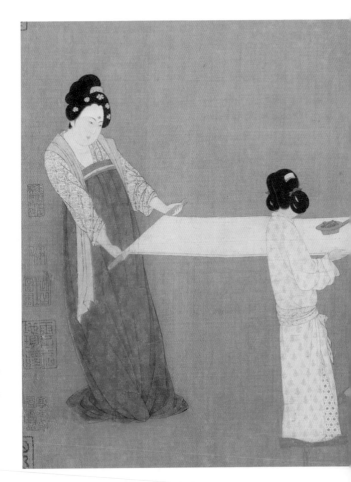

Yasodhara was a person who saw into people.

him at birth, and Yasodhara too was finding it hard to breathe in the closed-in air; she too was losing her belief in the dream. Inside their happiness was restlessness. This was a consequence of marrying someone who would take her out of the provincial enclosure of her life. She knew that he wanted to leave everything because she did, too.

While Yasodhara was pregnant, they were happy, but she, who wondered what was in people's minds, and who had the capacity to imagine what was to come, was troubled by dreams of parting. She went into labor and gave birth to a son. Siddhartha was amazed at how hard birth was, at the difficulties women go through—such a necessary human thing, yet it was so hard. Afterward, they were soft and close and exhilarated. They called the child Rahula, which means "fetter," because he bound them to desire, loss, and most of all to incompleteness.

It was a good day, but that night everything changed. The cause was an insignificant event. As usual, dancers and musicians were at the palace—and Siddhartha happened to walk past their quarters. The women were tired; their clothes had slipped off, and they lay in the sheen of dancing, sweat, and sex, deep in the innocence of sleep.

Siddhartha's father had designed a palace to be the fulfillment of every desire—a temple of distraction—and that evening, Siddhartha felt that the fulfillment of every desire was itself unbearably sad. He did not know what he longed for and knew that his longing never completed itself. "Ah," he thought, "my mind is crowded with thoughts, my life has no space or quiet, because it was designed to be that way; it was shaped to distract me."

Until that moment he had only accepted what was given. He had never spent even a single night outside the palace. In a swirl of grief and hope, he became convinced that a true life would be possible only if he left home. He was disgusted with himself; he couldn't help but want to flee, to breathe. Later he wondered if his father's thoroughly suffocating scheme was directing him to this discovery.

He looked in on his wife and newborn son. He saw them in the lamp light with a great intensity, as if nothing else were in the world. The baby, exhausted from his journey

With deep sorrow he turned away.[2]

into shape and form, opened his large eyes and looked at him, taking him in. The smell of milk and warmth was in the air. The birth of the child was the fifth touch, the final one. He could not bear the boy to grow up in his sequestered world, and in addition, a great force beyond anything he could imagine or control was at work. With deep sorrow he turned away.

It was many years before they were to meet again. When they did, Siddhartha's wife told their son to ask for his inheritance. Both Yasodhara and Rahula joined him and found for themselves what Siddhartha had discovered. Between the parting and the next meeting, Yasodhara lived in the palace and raised their child. Her life is described by the questions we ask about her.

Channa the chariot driver brought up the prince's great white horse, Kanthaka, as well as his own black mare. He wrapped their hooves with grass, muffling the sound. They mounted their horses like anyone setting off on a journey in the middle of the night, but the bridles did not ring nor the horses whinny. The earth spirits held up their hands. The horses stepped in silence from palm to palm, carrying the men secretly out of the palace and into the dark of the night.

They rode until the first birds called, the morning star grew pale, and the grey dawn came on. They had arrived at a place where hermits lived. Deer slept unafraid beneath the trees and birds fluttered at the travelers' feet. The prince took this for a sign. He dismounted and stretched, pausing for a moment before his new life began. He looked around at everything. Then he stripped off his rings and his gold bracelets and handed them to his most loved companion. He drew his sword and cut off his own long hair. He threw the locks into the air, and they didn't fall down. His sword he gave to his friend.

Channa wept and said, "How will I go back to the palace without you?"

"Death will part us all in the end, my oldest friend," said Siddhartha. "What am I to my mother now? The year turns and we have always known this day would come."

By chance encounter, a hunter came by and the prince traded his silk robes for the man's red, homespun linen.

He drew his sword and cut off his own long hair.

Channa turned for home, tears falling on the mare's neck; the white horse followed and he too wept great tears.

* * *

Siddhartha set out on his long road into everything unknown. At first he sought out reputable teachers and took on the practices they recommended.

He watched a hermit purify himself by fasting and enduring pain. He experimented with this practice; at this stage, he was happy simply to be trying a new path. It was far from the luxury of the palace and he liked that. It seemed to simplify matters, though other benefits were not obvious.

He realized it might be difficult to discover what he sought, so next he went to teachers who focused directly on the mind. The first one taught an ancient philosophical system that merged into a practice. Siddhartha learned to inquire into his thoughts and to notice that suffering ran all through the mind. He learned also to endure pain and to concentrate so deeply on an object, such as the breath, that all pain disappeared. He entered states in which there seemed to be no thought. His teacher invited him to stay and teach alongside him, but Siddhartha could tell that a small part of his heart was not at rest and he moved on, without knowing exactly what he was seeking.

The next teacher focused entirely on method. He taught Siddhartha to concentrate ever more deeply and subtly, to navigate those meditation states that had a form and could be remembered, and those that didn't.

Siddhartha's senses were cleansed—the green of the forest was green, green, green, and the sky became endlessly pure. Waking and sleeping were similar in an intriguing way; few thoughts stuck in his mind. When his body was in pain, his mind could remain clear, but whenever he stood up from meditating, his feelings often captured him and unhappiness would appear without warning.

Just when things seemed to be going well, disturbing thoughts would catch him off guard. He felt grief for the life he had left behind and annoyance at his companions. This wasn't a special, refined, spiritual unhappiness. It was

*The white horse followed
and he too wept great tears.*

the same dissatisfaction he had known in the palace. There
didn't seem to be a way to ward off something that was
unpredictable and apparently just part of being human. He
practiced sincerely, but at the end of every day, he felt he was
missing something, as if he had not completed a crucial task
he was meant to do.

As a last resort, and in desperation, he went to the
Kingdom of Magadha and became an ascetic. It was almost
giving up, but not quite. He lived naked and alone in the
ancient forests. He slept on a bed of thorns, ate a grain of
rice a day, and meditated in the charnel grounds where the
bodies were burned. He was lonely and sometimes he was
afraid. Wild animals came around the graveyards at night, but
they left him alone. He looked like a skeleton, and a group of
five other ascetics was impressed and took him as their leader.
They too had been rich and had left home. One day, near
starvation, Siddhartha fainted.

When he regained consciousness, he was alone and
discouraged, and began to think. The practices he had done
all went in the expected direction. Everything he did was like

the life he had left behind; his renunciation was full of desire and striving. He had become prince of the ascetics and he was also very tired.

"It's easy to feel ashamed of your life and to think that something must be done to feel worthy," he thought.

At this moment, he remembered the day when he was a child, under the rose apple tree. Everything was complete, sufficient, and without effort; a kind of freedom was already present beneath whatever was happening There was nothing to add, nothing to take away. And as his mind roamed around, a thought formed itself: "Perhaps this is the direction that leads to awakening." At the same time, an old question appeared: "Are you afraid of this happiness?"

"No," he thought, "no, I'm not afraid of this happiness."

Drifting in this way, Siddhartha fell asleep; he dreamed of space and vastness, and of his mother smiling. Then shapes appeared—he was climbing into the Himalayas and a temple there. A queen welcomed him, she gave him many teachings—the Heart Sutra among them, as well as other secrets that would remain hidden for centuries.

*His renunciation was full
of desire and striving.*

詔之寶積　江口遊君

即是普賢色身三昧

靈鷲常在宅

選仲母庚子寫出

*A queen welcomed him, she
gave him many teachings.*

象王背上
現婦女身
随縁不変
真如月影

旭胡井勝画顔寿筆画

He rose thinking, "Today I will awaken."

Meanwhile, in a nearby town, on the night of the full moon, a woman named Sujata also had a dream. The dream gave her a set of instructions. She didn't hesitate; she followed the instructions. She went out to her family's herd and milked a thousand cows. She fed the milk to five hundred cows, then, taking that milk, she fed it to two hundred and fifty cows, and so on down to the last eight cows. Then she took the condensed, rich milk from those last eight cows and mixed it with rice. She poured the milk rice into a golden bowl and walked out into the forest as the dream had told her to do. That's as much as she knew.

Siddhartha was sitting under a tree, having just awakened from his own dreams. He was so skinny and bony that Sujata thought he was the spirit of the tree. A faint light glowed from inside him. She smiled; she offered the bowl of milk rice, saying, "May this bring you as much happiness to eat as it has brought me to make." Siddhartha opened his eyes; she floated toward him shaking with joy and, catching her delight, he drank, breaking his fast of years.

He always remembered that meal. The milkmaid's gift and blessing were a return. Sujata was a force greater than his striving. This was the first time he had been defeated and that was promising. However, the ascetics he had been practicing with arrived just in time to see him receiving the bowl from Sujata. They had been his companions in austerity, and now they repudiated him. And so he was alone to face the coming night.

When he had finished eating, Siddhartha stood and stretched and walked to the riverbank. He was exhilarated. He waded in, and the water had a happy feel; it restored him. He threw the bowl into the river, saying, "If it floats upstream I will awaken this very night."

The golden bowl indeed floated against the current, disappearing upstream. It came to a place with ancient, overhanging trees and a waterfall with a whirlpool below it. There the bowl swirled around and around and was drawn down into the palace of the Black Snake Dragon King, an ancient being named Mahakala. The bowl sank down and down and banged lightly against seven other bowls,

She offered the bowl of milk rice, saying,
"May this bring you as much happiness
to eat as it has brought me to make."

making a dull clink. This was not really something new for the dragon, who had received bowls in just this way from the seven previous Buddhas. With a feeling for time that was slow and vast, the dragon thought that the most recent Buddha had died just the day before, and hearing the sound of the bowl, thought, "So soon," and was happy that a new Buddha was already about to appear. The bowl was received as a gift, and in this way someone else became a friend to Siddhartha.

After the heat of the day had passed, Siddhartha went back to his tree. On the way, he met a grass cutter, Sottiya, who gave him a bundle of soft, fragrant grass to sit on. Siddhartha went to the south side of the tree, but it was as if he stood at the hub of a great wheel and someone was treading on the rim—the earth sank to hell in front of him and rose up to heaven behind him. He moved to the west and the same thing happened, and it happened again in the north. But in the east, facing the direction of sunrise, he found the spot that did not move. He sat down on the immovable seat, vowing not to get up again until he had awakened. The light departed, trees and shapes became indistinct, the night came on, full of promise and danger.

Out of the twilight appeared Deva Putra Mara, the Chief of Demons, Seducer of Souls, Lord of Death, Dark King of the World of Form. When Siddhartha drank the rice milk, Mara had become fascinated by him and now attacked with all his horde.

Spears, fire arrows, and rocks fell from the air. The fire arrows turned into flowers and the stones into many colored lights. Fear itself became something to wonder at, something with its own beauty. Mara tried to seduce Siddhartha by offering lovely women to him. There were women who smiled and promised delight, women who needed him to rescue them, women who understood him so deeply that he was reminded of the mother he never knew, and he saw that they were all aspects of himself. Like his fear, desire and sorrow became freeing in themselves. Then a wild wind rose, and floods came; there was a shower of rocks, a shower of burning coals, and a shower of mud. But after fear and desire, these assaults were an afterthought.

Spears, fire arrows, and rocks fell from the air.

Mara's final strategy was argument. He challenged Siddhartha, asking, "By what right do you claim the seat on which you sit?" For Siddhartha, something unstoppable was unfolding. He didn't really care what questions he was asked. Mara continued, "I have my armies to bear witness for me," he said, "but who will speak for you?" Siddhartha's hand answered—almost out of courtesy, he reached down and touched the ground. The voice of the earth goddess, Bhumidevi, rose from below: "I can bear witness." The sun and the moon paused; the animals bowed. Mara howled and his howl diminished as he fled.

In the First Watch, the night proper began. Siddhartha went deeper into the vastness, into great silence, understanding many things. He remembered his childhood and the mother who gave birth to him. Then he remembered that he had lived before, remembered the first life, the second life, the third life, the fourth life, the tenth life, the twentieth life, the thirtieth life, the fortieth life, the fiftieth life, the hundredth life, the thousandth life, the hundred thousandth life, the countless formations of the universe, the countless destructions of the universe. He remembered what his given names had been, what his surnames were, what tribes he had belonged to, what he ate, what pleasures and sorrows he experienced. He remembered lives that were not his own and could see no significant difference. His life seemed to be a dream inside a dream.

In the Second Watch of the night, he understood cause and effect and the many realms of existence and rebirth: gods drifting in splendor, the wrathful gods fascinated and absorbed by war, animals, humans, hungry ghosts who are never satisfied, demons tormented in the depths of hell—he saw them all. Again he confirmed that there was no fixed substance in the universe and also nothing that does not change. He felt compassion for the suffering he witnessed. He saw that even Mara, the King of the Demons, was lonely and afraid of being without him.

In the Third Watch, the night deepened. The thoughts and stories from the day died down. It became obvious that everything is dependent on every other thing and has no nature apart from its relation to other things. Siddhartha

He reached down and
touched the ground.

He cried out, "I and all beings of the great Earth have at this moment attained the way."

could find no enduring self that needed to be protected or enhanced. He noticed his meditation had stages of ever deepening concentration and he explored them. He saw the noble truths: suffering, the cause of suffering, the end of suffering, and the path out of suffering.

In the Fourth Watch, it grew colder. The Hindu gods who had seen his birth returned to greet him. Flowers fell from the sky and just before dawn, the first birds called. Siddhartha looked up and saw the morning star and awakened. He cried out, "I and all beings of the great Earth have at this moment attained the way.

* * *

Siddhartha remained under the Bodhi tree for seven days, wanting nothing, feeling what had happened.

Then he said, "Life after life I looked for the builder of the house and could not find him. But now I can see you, builder! I have snapped the rafters and broken the ridge beam; I will not build this house of pain again.

"My mind is free of its conditions now. I am delivered, rebirth has ended, the true life is here, I have done what I set out to do.[3] As a flame blown out by the wind cannot be described, I am free from worries, the conditions that make the self."[4]

A great light spread out from the Bodhi tree; the sick were healed, the doors of prisons swung open, and even the recently dead were restored to life.

Now Mara returned. He argued that the Buddha should rest in the great peace he had found and avoid the world and the turmoil of other people. But the Black Snake Dragon King came to give protection, winding great coils underneath the Buddha as he sat, and raising seven hooded heads over him to shield him.

After he had sat for seven days, Siddhartha looked around and was filled with love for the world and its beings. He said, "This world is burning. What we want causes us to be afraid. We call our pain our self. We have things the wrong way round." And he was moved to leave his seat and go out to teach, beginning at the Deer Park with the five companions

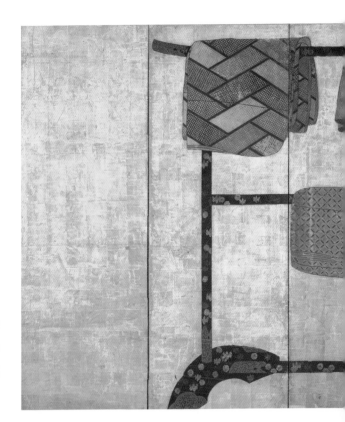

We call our pain our self. We have things the wrong way round.

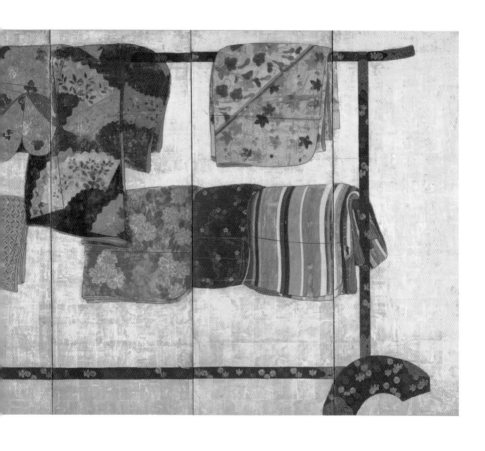

who had shared his austerities. After this, he was known as "The One Who Comes Thus," the Tathagata.

Siddhartha went on to become the Buddha and gave the teachings that can free anyone from suffering, even the people hearing this story. He had many interesting adventures, and his teaching was taken up and went to all the corners of the Earth and finally arrived in this room today. But all that is a story for another time.

Siddhartha went on to become the Buddha and gave the teachings that can free anyone from suffering, even the people hearing this story.

POSTSCRIPT
Keeping Company with the Story

Whenever I return to this story of awakening, a different image steps forward—the queen who dreams she is pregnant; the elephant with six tusks; the woman giving birth while holding a flowering branch; the loss of the mother; the grief-stricken king; the gods impersonating mortality; the friend who remains behind; the distressing purifications; the milkmaid who follows her own dreams; the golden bowl that does something impossible and travels upstream; the dragon, most ancient of beings, who welcomes the new Buddha; the voice of the goddess from deep in the earth; the torments that visit us at night; the lonely demon; the morning star. When the telling of the story is over, a piece is still in me. Observing which element steps forward is a practice of humility and intimacy; I let the story act on me without knowing what I will get in return.

As a girl, Marie-Louise von Franz met Carl Jung at a dinner party. He told a story about someone who went to the moon. Here is her account of that meeting.

> I said indignantly, "But she imagined herself to be on the moon, or she dreamt it, but she wasn't on the moon." And he looked at me earnestly and said, "Yes she was on the moon." I still remember looking over the lake and thinking, "Either this man is crazy, or I am too stupid to understand what he means." And then it suddenly dawned on me, "He means that what happens psychically is the real reality, and this other moon, this stony desert which goes around the Earth, that's illusion, or that's only pseudo-reality."[5]

When you hear the story of the Buddha, the part that touches you belongs to your psychic reality. It's an intersection, the place where your life rises to meet the Buddha's. It's *your* mother who dies, or *your* life that has closed in on you, or *your* horse who weeps. And because the story becomes personal and becomes yours, it opens a path that the teller hasn't imagined and you, the listener, were not expecting. The story is a vessel for the involuntary rising of images, and also a divination about what is happening for us now. If we listen to the images, we can tell where we are in life, where our course is taking us. With each telling, and hearing, we find ourselves in a different place in the journey.

* * *

This great Asian tradition—its stories and meditation teachings—took the long road from India over snowbound mountains and through immense deserts to China, where it became Chan and, in Japan, Zen. Chan became an art; the teachers offered stories, poems, questions, and surprises. When you studied with such a teacher, one of these stories went with you.

The Chan stories came to be called *koans*—a word that means "public cases leading to awakening." Koans did something unusual and paradoxical—they linked two meditation traditions. One tradition was of disbelief in the products of the mind, of throwing thoughts, feelings, views, overboard. The other tradition was more specifically creative—it involved telling stories and finding images that touch and change us, in ways that we don't control or even have to think about. The stories didn't try to impose an order on things, they let the universe speak for itself. Each story became a gate, and beyond it there was a path.

In Chan, the doctrine of the noble truths is replaced by the practice of directly pointing to the mind and heart. All by itself, the story turns into questions: "How do I see the mind?" "Who is wondering about the mind?" "What if we are already free?" "What is death?" "Is there a story that takes me out of the prison my mind makes with its stories?"—these become real questions to be engaged.

Here's a koan that was taken from the Buddha's life.

After meditating all night, Siddhartha looked up and saw the morning star and awakened. He cried out, "I and all beings of the great Earth have at this moment attained the way."[6]

The moment when the morning star appeared is a shard, a fragment that contains the whole story. And more, it's a fragment that contains the whole universe.

It's as if you are dreaming that you are in prison, unbearably confined. Naturally you want to do things to get you out, but of course that won't work. It's the mind that is in prison, and its movement is the thing, not the conclusions it comes to. Asking questions and wanting to escape from prison are just the nature of mind. You don't need hacksaws or helicopters or disguises or even good behavior to get out of the prison. To get free, you turn, you enter the suffering, you see that the suffering itself is part of a dream.

It's liberating to be curious about our lives and to learn our own moves. We live by our thoughts and suffer them, but on examination, they do not appear in any sense to be ours. And so, for me, the story gives an image of the way we are connected to something larger than ourselves, a great part of existence that is often ignored or invisible and yet which, even so, carries us along. We have intimations, feelings, and images that lead inside, beyond, or beneath our day-world, and even a glimpse of a deeper life makes a difference to our outlook. We remember such moments and we look for them and they change us.

We do not have the life that we planned or that was planned for us. In the gaps between there is often sorrow, yet there is also surprise and a fierce wonder. The original silence is always reappearing, and when it does, we feel how we belong in the world and are at home.

MEDITATIONS ABOUT
THE BUDDHA'S LIFE

To pass through this story is to make a pilgrimage—I have found that the waystations of the legend in some way describe and illuminate my own life. My own restlessness and unease became recognizably part of a spiritual search.

When I first heard about the Buddha's life, the extremity of the departures and losses struck me, as did their repetitions; Siddhartha lost his mother when he was a baby, and in turn he abandoned his own son, his wife, his realm. I was always disturbed by this sacrifice.

I never quite fit with my own, Tasmanian, culture, or perhaps any culture—I couldn't find a ready-to-wear outfit. After a succession of improvisations—working in a smelter, working on a fishing boat, working for land rights—I realized my question was an inner one: "Who am I?" was one way to put it. Just asking began a movement to enter the inexplicable in my life; the question was as valuable as an answer. On night shift in the smelter, I watched the peacock-colored fires and sometimes fell into a state in which they were inside as well as outside. The distance that I felt from the objects around me, and from myself, suddenly vanished. Briefly, momentarily, I had a place under the aspect of eternity.

So, without knowing anything about the Dharma, I set off to study Zen. I left my country, my work, and most of my friends, and entered a monastery. In this departure, the imperative to leave home, as in the Buddha's story, became natural, archetypal—the beginning of the journey proper.

In the final piece of his story, the Buddha, having sat all night under a great fig tree, is attacked by Mara, the Lord of Death, and his legions, facing terrors and longings I was personally familiar with.

Everybody in our temple worked hard to awaken, but the effort was full of, well, effort. I was trying to find freedom but even my quest was full of desire.

There was the matter, too, of the children. Siddhartha abandoning his son on the night of his birth touched me. The night my daughter was born, she rested on my chest, and the tenderness of her skin seemed to be a mystery beyond the stars. She and I were both included in that pattern, along with her mother, the doctors and nurses, and the scent of plum blossoms through the open window.

As my daughter grew, I took her with me when I traveled to teach retreats. The idea was that we would have to have silence, peace, and awakening in the middle of the disorder of life—the modern monastery could include children; it had to be possible, I thought. Other children came to retreats, too. They would take cut lunches and hurtle off up the creeks, coming back in time for supper.

My story did relate to the Buddha's: The correspondence was what in poetry is called a half rhyme.

There's a true connection, but it's not identical—it's not *love* and *dove*, it's *love* and *stove*. On my way to teach a retreat, I carried my infant daughter onto an airliner, and she wailed all the way across the Pacific in the bulkhead bassinet. It's as if when I left the palace, even though the spirits tried to help me steal away, she made all the noise in the world. So that's how we left the palace—together. A steward, saying "It's hard to have a nipper," secretly passed me a bottle of champagne from first class. He was like the milkmaid in the Buddha's story, offering blessing and nourishment.

I found that many places in the Buddha's story opened to me, and the journey itself was a resting place. It came alive when the light seemed not to play line by line on the narrative and its destination, but to strike the shards, the particular moments.

The intelligent thread of instructions, all I had learned at the monastery—this is how to do it and what to sacrifice, and this is where you'll end up—was reasonable and even respectable. But my mind was not reasonable or respectable. When we walk the pilgrimage of the Buddha's life, we find that the destination is wholeness, not purity. It must include the life we already have, and, in addition, it has an incomplete, unknowable element. The light is in the leaves and the tips of the grass, in the feelings as well as the thoughts, all scattered about. Anywhere—I can enter the Buddha's story anywhere. Here is always good.

* * *

Here are some meditations related to the Buddha's story, each of them a glimpse into how the ancestors of the Zen tradition found their own gates into the pilgrimage and discovered awakening for themselves. The questions that arise, along with our involuntary responses, connect our own lives to the mystery the Buddha sought to understand.

You will discover how to meditate with the koans just by valuing the time you spend with them—meditation teaches meditation. Don't try to use it to achieve something. Just hold the story in mind, or any part of the story. Stay with it day and night. It's not so hard.

The light is in the leaves and the tips of the grass, in the feelings as well as the thoughts.

The first koan you are already familiar with, and it became part of the Zen canon. For each story I have included a poem or fragment by another master. Sometimes these are by tradition linked, sometimes not. It is true that the meditation path is creative. A saying and an insight might appear only for you. You, too, build the tradition. Here is a different version from another old sacred text. Here we go.

I.

After meditating all night, Siddhartha looked up and saw the morning star and awakened. He cried out, "I and all beings of the great Earth have at this moment attained the way."

> The old plum tree puts out a flowering branch,
> Thorns grow on it eventually.
> —KEIZAN JOKIN

Again and again we return to this fragment of the story, since it is the exemplary moment when all that might be hoped for becomes possible. In the flowering plum is the whole of spring. Thoughts come and go, too. The blossoms and the thorns, is there anything wrong with this life?

2.

A student asked Zhaozhou, "Does a dog have Buddha nature or not?"

Zhaozhou said, "*No.*"

Dog, Buddha nature—
completely manifesting it all.
With one instant of "has" or "doesn't have"
you lose your life.[7]
—WUMEN HUIKAI

If I watch a bird or a dog or a kangaroo, it seems obvious that every creature has a marvelous life, a quality the old teachers called "Buddha nature." Each being seems complete in the vastness of galaxies, even creatures we might disregard.

3.

A student asked great ancestor Mazu.

"What is Buddha?"

Mazu said, "Your thoughts and feelings are Buddha."

The sky is blue, the day bright —
you don't have to search around.
"What is Buddha?" you ask.
you hide the loot in your pocket and call
        yourself innocent.[8]

—WUMEN HUIKAI

Everything you meet contains the whole meaning of your life. This life we have now, without improvement or self-help, is already complete and in its own way, perfect.

4.

Are you afraid of this happiness?

> This place is paradise,
> This body, the Buddha.[9]
> —HAKUIN EKAKU

This is the only moment, and this is the only place we have. We can't reject it, but we can be grateful, and welcoming, and truly have our lives. What treasure is hidden in your body?

5.

The baby Buddha's skin was golden, and the moment after birth, he took seven steps. With one hand he pointed to the sky and with the other to the earth, saying, "Above heaven and beneath the earth, there is only I, eldest and first, alone and sacred."

Yunmen, with his whole body and mind, served infinite worlds. This is known as paying back the Buddha's benevolence.

Yunmen said, "If I'd been there, I would have killed him with my staff and fed him to the dogs. It's important that the world be at peace."

Langye Huijue commented, "Yunmen, with his whole body and mind, served infinite worlds. This is known as paying back the Buddha's benevolence."[10]

Every baby is the ruler of the world when she is born. Still, the mystery is different from making philosophy about the mystery. Yunmen likes that which is real. He thinks we can have a real peace that has a modesty, and everyone, of royal birth or not, can move in that direction. How does even a child enter the mystery?

6.

Siddhartha went to the south side of the tree, but it was as
if he stood at the hub of a great wheel and someone was
treading on the rim—the earth sank to hell in front of him
and rose up to heaven behind him. He moved to the west and
the same thing happened, and it happened again in the north.
But in the east, facing the direction of sunrise, he found the
spot that did not move.

> When you take the role of host
> Your place will be a true one[11]
> —LINJI YIXUAN

Wherever you sit, wherever you stand, on a bus, on a plane,
what is your immoveable spot?

Facing the direction of sunrise, he found the spot that did not move.

When you take the role of host,
your place will be a true one.

7.

A student asked Yunmen,

"What is Buddha?"

Yunmen replied, "Dried shit stick!"

A flash of lightning,
sparks struck from flint,
if you blink,
it's already gone.[12]

—WUMEN HUIKAI

And just in case we were getting pure and perfect about this, we have the grandmaster Yunmen once again emphasizing that everything to do with being is included. If you believe in things outside yourself, you separate yourself. Is there anything in your life that is left out from Buddha nature?

8.

Once, in ancient times, when the World-Honored One was at Vulture Peak, he twirled a flower before the assembled students. Everyone was silent. Only Mahakasyapa broke into a smile.

The World-Honored One said, "I have the eye of the real teachings, the wonderful mind of nirvana, the form without form, and the mysterious gate of the teaching. It doesn't rely on words and sayings. It is a special transmission beyond words. Now I pass this on to Mahakasyapa."

> He holds up a flower,
> the snake shows its tail.
> Mahakasyapa breaks into a smile,
> no one there knows what to do.[13]
> —WUMEN HUIKAI

If you see the tail, the whole snake is somewhere about. Each piece of the cosmos is the whole of the cosmos. A flower is enough. What is the tail, today? This is a legend of the first

If you blink, it's already gone.

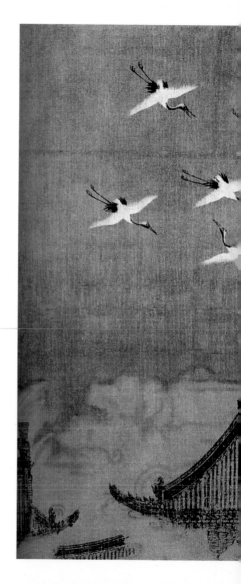

Each piece of the cosmos is the whole of the cosmos.

time the Zen teachings were passed on from the Buddha to one of his students. You can tell that the smile is an indication of meeting and understanding.

* * *

The Zen idea is that the teaching is passed on directly from mind to mind: Holding up a flower will do. Any encounter is a true encounter.

* * *

It seems that the Buddha's story completes itself in our own lives. The mystery gets handed over to us, and now it is our turn to pass on the teachings to the children and to the generations to come in whatever world is available to them. No other way exists; there is no other Buddha apart from you and me.

There is no other Buddha
apart from you and me.

新都橋の白雨

御竹藏の虹

神とさと
かくる
萬を驚く
柳とて
みちの野
勢とも
ぬらさ
みさち

梯子

ACKNOWLEDGMENTS

Nikko Odiseos envisioned the book and suggested adding illustrations.

The team at Shambhala was great—Tasha Kimmet shepherded the book and Peter Schumacher gave a surprisingly attentive look at the text.

Allison Atwill was my constant editor. She and Corey Hitchcock looked through the vaults of great museums and came out with the images to use.

This story was a project of many years at Pacifc Zen Institute. Everyone at retreats who walked and meditated the Buddha story with me helped to develop it.

NOTES

1. *Blue Cliff Record*, trans. Joan Sutherland and John Tarrant (unpublished translation), case 36.

2. This image from Sarnath of the Buddha leaving home, or "the Great Departure" as it is often called, is unusual. Sarnath is in India, but the image looked Japanese, so my editor Allison Atwill investigated. She found that the frescoes of Mulagandha Kuti Vihara temple in Sarnath were created by the renowned Japanese artist Kosetsu Nosu. As a Buddhist with an intimate connection to Indian arts, Kosetsu Nosu was selected to make a mural painting on the life of Lord Buddha at the Mulagandha Kuti Vihara temple in 1931. The

wall paintings were finished in 1936, five years after the temple construction was completed. The image of Sujata offering milk on page 63 is also from Kosetsu Nosu's Sarnath murals.

Over the years the murals started deteriorating—preservation work began in 2019 and was completed in 2023 by a team of Japanese master artists. For the restoration the team replicated the original paint used by Kosetsu Nosu.

3. Dhammapada, trans. John Tarrant (unpublished translation), stanzas 153–54. This is a famous saying of the Buddha from the Pali canon recorded by Ananda, the Buddha's attendant and one of his foremost disciples who is believed to have memorized the Buddha's oral teachings.

4. "A flame blown out" is an image for the disappearance of the self that appears many times in the Pali canon's descriptions of nirvana, which literally means "blowing

out," as in a candle. The Chan or Zen image for awakening is that a candle passes its light to another candle with no loss of the original light.

5. *Matter of Heart: The Extraordinary Journey of C. G. Jung*, directed by Mark Whitney, written by Suzanne Wagner (1986). This film about Carl Jung's circle and ideas opens with an interview with Marie-Louise von Franz in which she tells the story of the woman who lived on the moon.

6. Keizan, *Denkoroku: The Transmission of the Light*, trans. Joan Sutherland and John Tarrant (unpublished translation), case 1.

7. Wumen Huikai, *Gateless Barrier*, trans. Joan Sutherland and John Tarrant (unpublished translation), case 1.

8. Wumen Huikai, *Gateless Barrier*, trans. Joan Sutherland and John Tarrant (unpublished translation), case 30.

9. Hakuin Ekaku, "Praise Song for Meditation," trans. Joan Sutherland and John Tarrant (unpublished translation).

10. *Entangling Vines: A Classic Collection of Zen Koans*, trans. Thomas Yuho Kirchner (Somerville, MA: Wisdom Publications, 2013), case 114.

11. *The Linji Lu: The Record of Linji*, trans. Joan Sutherland and John Tarrant.

12. Wumen Huikai, *Gateless Barrier*, trans. Joan Sutherland and John Tarrant (unpublished translation), case 21.

13. Wumen Huikai, *Gateless Barrier*, trans. Joan Sutherland and John Tarrant (unpublished translation), case 6. This story first appears in China and is an illustration of the way Buddhist teachings turned into stories and images as they came east.

IMAGE CREDITS

The images have been chosen mainly from Chinese and Japanese sources to give some unity to the selection and also to illustrate how differently Buddhism developed in China and Japan.

Page 3: Buddha Preaching the Law. China, Dunhuang, Mogao Cave 17. 701–750 CE. Ink and colors on silk. 163.3 x 121.5 cm. The British Museum, 1919,0101,0.6. License: © The Trustees of the British Museum.

Page 4: Tani Bunchō (Japanese, 1763– 840). Dragon in clouds. Japan. 19th century. Hanging scroll painting. 119.9 x 177.3 cm. The British Museum, 1934,0714,0.1. License: © The Trustees of the British Museum.

Page 13: Detail. Tawaraya Sōtatsu (Japanese, 1570–1643). The Wind and Thunder Gods (Fūjin and Raijin). Japan. 17th century. Painted folding screens; ink and color on gold-foiled paper. 169.8 x 154.5 cm, each. Kyoto National Museum (owned by Ninna-ji temple). Public Domain, via Wikimedia Commons.

Pages 16–17: Scene from The Illustrated Sutra of Past and Present Karma (Kako genzai e-inga-kyō; Matsunaga Version). Japan. Late 13th century. Handscroll; ink and color on paper. 27.8 x 156.5 cm. The Metropolitan Museum of Art, Mary Griggs Burke Collection, Gift of the Mary and Jackson Burke Foundation, 2015, 2015.300.7. Public Domain, CC0.

Pages 22–23: Detail of the Dream of Queen Maya. Four scenes from the Life of the Buddha. China, Dunhuang, Mogao Cave 17. 9th century. Painted banner; ink and colors on silk. 60 x 16.5 cm. The British Museum, 1919,0101,0.96. License: © The Trustees of the British Museum.

Page 27: Hanegawa Chincho (Japanese, 1679?–1754). Birth of the Buddha. Japan. c. 1710. Hand-colored woodblock print; vertical o-oban, tan-e. 50.8 x 27.1 cm. The Art Institute of Chicago, Kate S. Buckingham Endowment, 1966.163. Public Domain, CC0.

Page 35: Detail of Shakyamuni seeing a sick man. Banner fragment with two scenes from the Life of the Buddha, showing two of the Four Encounters. China, Dunhuang, Mogao Cave 17. c. 701–850. Banner; ink and color on silk. 56 x 40.7 cm (overall, in mount). The British Museum, 1919,0101,0.88. License: © The Trustees of the British Museum.

Pages 40–41: Detail. Attributed to Emperor Huizong (Chinese, 1082–1135). Court Ladies Preparing Newly Woven Silk. China. Northern Song dynasty, early 12th century. Ink, color, and gold on silk. 37.7 x 466 cm (overall). The Museum of Fine Arts, Boston, Chinese and Japanese Special Fund, 12.886. Public Domain, via Wikimedia Commons.

Page 45: Flight from the Palace (detail). Kosetsu Nosu (Japanese, 1885–1973). Life of the Buddha murals in the Mulagandha Kuti Vihara, Sarnath, India. 1936. 4.3 x 44 m. Photograph reproduced with permission of Kevin Standage Photography.

Page 49: Prince Gautama cutting his hair. China. Ming dynasty, 1368–1644. Wall painting fragment; ink and color on plaster. 24 x 26 x 1.8 cm. The British Museum, 1936,1009,0.87. License: © The Trustees of the British Museum.

Pages 52–53: Detail showing Shakyamuni's farewell to his groom Chandaka and his horse Kanthaka. Three Scenes from the Life of the Buddha. China, Dunhuang, Mogao Cave 17. 8th–9th century. Painted banner; ink and color on silk. 58.5 x 18.5 cm (painted image). The British Museum, 1919,0101,0.97. License: © The Trustees of the British Museum.

Page 57: Minamoto Masakatsu (Japanese). Emaciated Shaka After Fasting. Japan. 1630. Gilded and lacquered bronze. 37.8 x 29 x 24.5 cm. The British Museum, 1891,0905.20. License: © The Trustees of the British Museum.

Pages 58–59: Katsukawa Shunshō (Japanese, 1726–1792). Courtesan of Eguchi. Japan. 1770–1780; inscribed 1820s–1830s by Butsumo Keisen (Japanese, 1771–1854). Hanging scroll; ink and color on paper. 37.8 x 51.9 cm (image). The Metropolitan Museum of Art, Mary and Cheney Cowles Collection, Gift of Mary and Cheney Cowles, 2018, 2018.853.26. Public Domain, CC0.

Page 63: Sujata offering rice milk to the Buddha (detail). Kosetsu Nosu (Japanese, 1885–1973). Life of the Buddha murals in the Mulagandha Kuti Vihara, Sarnath, India. 1936. 4.3 x 44 m. Photograph reproduced with permission of Kevin Standage Photography.

Page 67: Scene from the Life of the Buddha: The Submission of Mara. China, Duhuang, Mogao Caves. First half of the 10th century. Painting on silk. 144.4 x 113 cm. Musée Guimet, Paris, Pelliot Mission, MG 17655. Public Domain, via Wikimedia Commons.

Page 71: The Jina Buddha Ratnasambhava. Central Tibet (by a Newar artist). c. 1100–1125. Mineral pigments and gold on cotton cloth. 40.96 x 33.02 cm. The Los Angeles County Museum of Art, From the Nasli and Alice Heeramaneck Collection, purchased with funds provided by the Jane and Justin Dart Foundation, M.81.90.5. Public Domain.

Pages 72–73: Sakai Hōitsu (Japanese, 1761–1828). Blossoming Cherry Trees. Japan. c. 1805. Pair of six-panel folding screens; ink, color, and gold leaf on paper. 96.5 x 208.8 cm (image). The Metropolitan Museum of Art, Mary Griggs Burke Collection, Gift of the Mary and Jackson Burke Foundation, 2015, 2015.300.93.1, .2. Public Domain, CC0.

Pages 76–77: Tagasode ("Whose Sleeves?"). Japan. First half of the 17th century. Pair of six-panel folding screens; ink, color, gold, silver, and gold leaf on paper. 150.5 x 332 cm (overall, each screen). The Metropolitan Museum of Art, H. O. Havemeyer Collection, Gift of Mrs. Dunbar W. Bostwick, John C. Wilmerding, J. Watson Webb Jr., Harry H. Webb, and Samuel B. Webb, 1962, 62.36.2, .3. Public Domain, CC0.

Pages 80–81: The Teaching of Buddha Sakyamuni. Zhang Shengwen. Scroll of Buddhist Images. China. 12th century (c. 1173–1176). Scroll; ink and color on paper. 30.4 x 1,636.5 cm. Photograph from National Palace Museum. Image number K2A001003N000000000PAO. Public Domain, CC BY-4.0:

Page 95: Suzuki Harunobu (Japanese, 1725–1770). Saigyō Hōshi Praying to a Bijin on a White Elephant. Japan. c. 1766. Woodblock print; ink and color on paper. 27.1 x 19.5 cm. Honolulu Museum of Art, Gift of James A. Michener, 1970, 15554. Public Domain, via Wikimedia Commons.

Page 101: Detail. Koizumi Junsaku (Japanese, 1924–2012). Twin Dragons. Hondo Hall, Kennin-ji Zen Temple, Kyoto, Japan. 2002. Ceiling painting; ink on paper. 11.4 x 15.7 m. License: Adam Jones from Kelowna, BC, Canada, CC BY-SA 2.0, via Wikimedia Commons.

Pages 104–5: Kano Sansetsu (Japanese, 1590–1651). Old Plum. Japan. 1646. Four sliding-door panels (fusuma); ink, color, gold, and gold leaf on paper. 174.6 x 485.5 cm (overall of all four panels). The Metropolitan Museum of Art, The Harry G. C. Packard Collection of Asian Art, Gift of Harry G. C. Packard, and Purchase, Fletcher, Rogers, Harris Brisbane Dick, and Louis V. Bell Funds, Joseph Pulitzer Bequest, and The Annenberg Fund Inc. Gift, 1975, 1975.268.48a-d. Public Domain, CC0.

Page 107: Detail. Hakuin Ekaku (Japanese, 1685-1768). Portrait of Rinzai. Japan. About 1750 (Edo period). Vertical hanging scroll; ink and light color on paper. 51 7/8 x 21 ¾ in. (image); 81 5/8 x 26 5/8 in. (overall). Indianapolis Museum of Art at

Newfields, The Ballard Fund, Deaccessioned Asian Art, and Asian Art Discretionary Fund, 2008.363. Public Domain.

Page 111: Detail of Yunmen. Kenko Shokei (Japanese, c. 1480-c. 1518). Encounter of Yun-men Wen-yen and Fa-yen Wen-i. Japan. 1473-1523 (Muromachi period). Color and gold on paper. 49.1 x 39.4 cm. Smithsonian National Museum of Asian Art, Freer Gallery of Art Collection, Gift of Charles Lang Freer, F1905.266a-b. Public Domain, CC0.

Pages 112–13: Emperor Huizong of Song (Chinese, 1082–1135). Auspicious Cranes. China. 1112. Handscroll; ink and color on silk. Liaoning Provincial Museum. Public Domain, via Wikimedia Commons.

Pages 116–17: Katsushika Hokusai (Japanese, 1760–1849). Shower at the New Yanagi Bridge. Japan. 1806. Woodblock print; ink and color on paper. 20 x 29.8 cm. The Metropolitan Museum of Art, The Howard Mansfield Collection, Purchase, Rogers Fund, JP2580. Public Domain, CC0.

ABOUT THE AUTHOR

John Tarrant is the director of Pacific Zen Institute (pacifczen.org). Originally from Tasmania, he has a PhD in psychology and for many years had a practice in Jungian dream analysis. He has taught at a number of medical schools, including Duke University and the University of Arizona at Tucson. His deep interest is in the integration of Zen koan work, the arts, and the imagination.